Daito-ryu
Aikijujutsu
Martial Art of Samurais

by *Ostap Vereshko, Yasuhiro Odzawa*

The book discovers secrets of **Daito-ryu Aikijujutsu** technique – a style that is an origin of Aikido – a famous and popular type of martial arts for the first time. The work describes in detail the main technique of the school, presents information about the history, philosophy and psychophysical aspects of Daito-ryu.

The book contains the large number of illustrations with detail presentation of peculiarities of the style technique and will be useful for all, who studies martial arts.

© 2018, Dudukchan I.M.
All Rights reserved.
Authors: Ostap Vereshko, Yasuhiro Odzawa
Translator: Elena Novitskaja
ISBN: 9781719847179

Contents:

Introduction
Generation and formation of Daito-ryu Aikijujutsu

Sokaku Takeda
(1859-1943)

The famous military leader and one of descendants of the emperor Seiwa, **Shinra Saburo Minamoto no Yoshimitsu**, is acknowledged as a creator of **Daito-ryu Aikijujutsu**. Due to the serious study of the human anatomy, he succeeded in determining and classifying the effectiveness of blows, throws and pain holds and created different combinations of techniques.

Yoshimitsu transmitted his system of martial art to his sons, and it was further named Daito-Ryu in honor of one of residences of the clan.

Yoshiki Yo, the older son of Minanoto, settled in the village **Takeda** in Koma (Yamanashi prefecture) and founded the branch of Takeda.

Takeda clan, inherited Yoshimitsu knowledge, continuously developed and improved them as a secret family martial art, known as «**Takeda no Heiho**».

At the end of sixteenth century one of Takeda family – **Kanitsugu**, had created a new branch of Takeda clan in Aizu province (Fukushima prefecture), where this type of single combats became to be called "**O-Shiki-Uchi**" – exercises in the room, or **O-Tome-Bujutsu** – intra-clan martial art». This system was transmitted as a rigorous secret to samurais from Aizu estate to the point of Shougunate decline in 1868.

As a result of reforms of **Meiji** government, the country division in independent domains had been cancelled, and many schools, hold by local feudal lords, remained without patrons. It forced many patriarchs to begin to teach secrets of their family styles to a wide circle of interested persons.

Thus, the first, who began to teach Aikijujutsu free, was **Sokaku Takeda**, who kept all secrets of **Daito-ryu** art.

Sokaku Takeda was born in Aizu province at 10 of October, 1859. He was taught **Jujutsu** by his grandfather **Soemon Takeda**, and his father gave him knowledge of **Bo-Jutsu** – fencing with poles. In Tokyo Sokaku trained the sword art of **Ono-ha-Itto-ryu** school under the guidance of **Toma Shibuya**, and **Jikishinkage-ryu** with **Kenkichi Sakakibara**.

In June of 1886 the older brother of Sokaku Takeda died, that forced him to return to **Aizu** and favored his acquaintance with the head of the clan, **Tanomo Saigo**. The latter taught him **Daito-ryu Aiki-Bujutsu** – a complex martial system, included **Nage-Waza** (throws), **Osae-Waza** (holdings), **Torae-Waza** (grips), **Batto-Jutsu** (snatching of a sword with a synchronous blow), **Yari-Jutsu** (javelin mastership) and many other. Tanomo Saigo transmitted all his knowledge to a talented pupil, including **Daito-ryu Aiki-Bujutsu** secret techniques.

From 1880 to 1898 Sokaku Takeda travelled throughout the country, competing with any master of Budo, who had enough courage to take a dare. At that all combats were conducted by a weapon, mastered by an opponent. It is supposed that all Sokaku's opponents were defeated due to the filigree technique of the talented master. At the same time he won numerous fights with different criminal contingent, where combats were conducted without any rules, often by a crowd against one. Having the full and interesting life, Sokaku Takeda died naturally at 25 of April, 1943.

Sokaku Takeda's official successor was his third son – **Tokimune Takeda**. After his death in 1993 **Katsuyuki Kondo** – the main instructor of Daito-kan was acknowledged as a keeper of the tradition.

The adoptee of Sokaku Takeda – **Shiro Saigo**, had moved to Nagasaki and taught Aikijujutsu there.Today this branch is called **Saigo-ha Daito-ryu**.

Kodo Horikawa (1895-1980) began to practice Daito-ryu with his father, then with the Great Master himself. Horikawa lived his whole life at Hokkaido, where he spread Daito-ryu doctrine. The most famous and outstanding of his pupils was Okamoto Shogo.

Takuma Hisa (1896-1980) was the most devoted Daito-ryu's pupil from the Western Japan and spread this system in Osaka district.

The one of most famous Sokaku Takeda's pupils was **Morihei Ueshiba**, who at the end of 40-ies created his own interpretation of Daito-ryu Aikijutsu, named **Aikido**.

The one most famous pupil of the master Sokaku was a Korean **Choi Yon Sul**, who after studying Aikijutsu and returning home, created the famous **Hapkido** style, that is was a successful alloy of Daito-ryu Aikijujutsu techniques with local holds of kicks and weapon.

Minoru Mochizuki had learnt Aikido with Morihei Ueshiba, **Judo** with Jigoro Kano, **Karate-do** with Gichin Funakoshi and created his direction of martial arts, named **Yoseikan Aiki-Budo**.

It is necessary to say that the founder of **Kyokushinkai Karate-do**, **Masutatsu Oyama** also trained holds of **Daito-ryu Aikijujutsu**.

Thus, we can see that Daito-ryu Aikijujutsu art continues to develop just in Japan and remarkably influences other types of martial arts throughout the world.

This book described the technique, peculiarities and principles of classic Daito-ryu Aikijujutsu, Tokimune Takeda line for the first time.

Technique and training methods in Daito-ryu Aikijujutsu

Today Daito-ryu remains a little-known school of classic Budo, so there is a great deficit of information as to technical aspects of the system and its training methods.

This book briefly presents nuances relating to these themes.

At first, it is necessary to know that all main knowledge in the tactics, technique and strategy of the school are transmitted as lists – Mokuroku.

Daito-ryu Aikibudo contains six lists:

1. *Hidden Mokuroku*,
2. *Aiki no Jutsu Mokuroku*,
3. *Chuden Mokuroku*,
4. *Goshin yo no te Mokuroku*,
5. *Soden Mokuroku*,
6. *Okuden Mokuroku* (*This list is transmitted only to people of higher initiation– Menkyo Kaiden*).

Chapter 1
Base techniques

Kamae – stances

Two main stances are usually used in Aikijutsu: **Hanmi** (stance position) and **Seiza** (knee position).

Hanmi stance is a base one, at which the fighter's body takes the three-side pyramid shape, wide in the base and narrow in the top. It gives stability and allows to move easily in any direction. The feet position and look focus are important.

The feet are perpendicularly to each other. The distance between them must be one and a half foot. Near 70% on the body weight is on the rear leg. The right arm is raised at the breast level, the elbow is directed down and a bit bent. The rear hand is at the belly level in ten centimeters from the body. Fingers are a bit apart and directed forward. The look is concentrated on the point between the adversary's eyes (fig.1).

1

Seiza position (knee stance) is an ideal stance for training a combat in pair.

Lower from Migi-Hanmi position (right-side stance) down by the whole body, lowering the left knee on the ground besides the right heel. Place the right foot besides the left one and lower your hips in such a way that both knees lean against the ground. Place both hands on the hips. Move the knees forward and seat fully on the shin and feet. Straighten your spine, lower your shoulders. You are in Seiza position (fig.2-6).

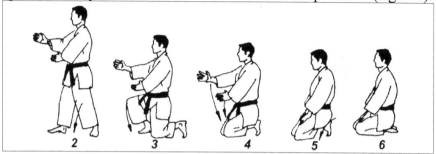

Shikkyo – the shift on knees

Aikijujutsu contains many techniques, executed from seating on the knees. The importance of studying techniques in the seating position (**Suwari-Waza**) is that together with developing the low extremities they train a pupil to studying techniques, executed in the standing position (**Tachi-Waza**).

The base method of forward-back movement at seating on the knees is presented to readers' attention.

Raise your hips from Seiza position. Lower the left knee, rotate on the right knee, and move feet by 90 degrees clockwise, keeping the knees together. Thus, you have made the step forward. Without raising the right knee, lower the left one on the ground.   Use your left knee as a rotating point, raise your right knee and move the feet by 90 degrees to the right (counterclockwise), in such a way making the next step forward. The hands easily touch the hips, the look is directed forward (fig.7-11).

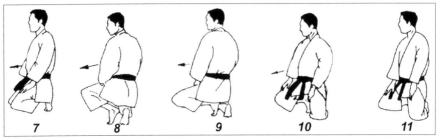

7 8 9 10 11

Ukemi – the safety technique at falling

Ukemi – is a method of body protection from injuries at falling at making throws. Techniques, related to this method, allow to avoid traumas at training and in real situations.

This work presents two main types of Ukemi: safety at falling back and safety at falling forward.

Safety at falling back

Squat, bending your knees and lowering your hips down. Synchronously straighten the arms forward at the shoulder level. Bend your spine and place your buttocks as close to the heels as possible. Overturn back, keeping your spine in the bent position. The chin must be pressed to the breast. Both arms remain relaxed, but strike the ground with force. Without straining your hips, allow the body to swing farther towards the inertia force. The chin must be pressed to the breast to save the nape from striking the ground (fig.12-15).

12 13 14 15

Safety at falling forward

Bend forward down, lower the right hand on the ground and move the body weight forward. Roll the body forward over the shoulder. The chin is pressed to the breast. At the end of the roll strike the ground by the left hand. At the moment of touching the floor the right leg must be bent at the angle of 90 degrees. Using the movement inertia, take the vertical position, ready to resist any attack (fig.16-19).

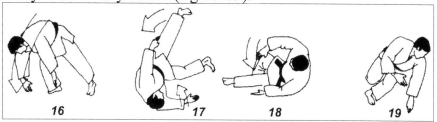

Blows in Aikijujutsu

The main weapon in Daito-ryu Aikijujutsu is grips, throws and pain controls. But blows as components of the aforesaid technical actions cannot be underestimated. Here blows are stricken for distracting attention before making a throw or grip and also as finishing actions in practically all forms. Base methods of striking blows will be considered in this book.

Tsuki – the direct blow by the fist

This blow can be stricken directly by the fist and also by the bent forefinger phalanx, extended forward. It can be stricken by both lead and rear arms. The aim of the attack is usually vulnerable points on the human body, such as the throat, eyes, armpit, solar plexus (fig.20, 21).

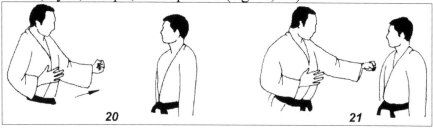

Shomen Uchi
– the direct blow by the palm rib from above

The striking surface moves along the maximally vertical trajectory. The aim of the attack is the collarbone, shoulder joint, extremities, throat and so on. It is necessary to keep fingers of the striking arm grouped and pressed to each other (fig.22, 23).

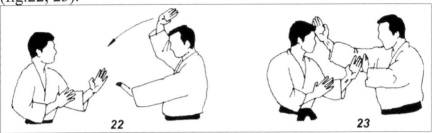

22   23

Yokomen Uchi

The striking surface of the arm moves top-down along the tangential trajectory. So, you can beat on the adversary's temple, ear, neck, extremities, ribs (fig.24, 25).

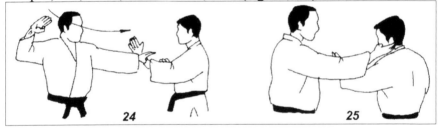

24   25

Chapter 2
Daito-ryu Aikijujutsu main techniques

Daito-ryu Aikijujutsu main technique includes one hundred eighteen holds of Hidden Mokuroku. This set of holds is divided in five groups:
-**Ikkajo** (first group) – 30 techniques,
-**Nikajo** (second group) – 30 techniques,
- **Sankajo** (third group) – 30 techniques,
-**Yonkajo** (fourth group) – 15 techniques,
-**Gokajo** (fifth group) – 13 techniques.

In its turn each of these groups is divided in four ones:
-**Tachiai** – holds, made in the face to face stance,
-**Idori** – holds, made face to face on the knees,
-**Hanza-Handachi** – holds, made, when an attacking person is in the stance, and a defending one on the knees,
- **Ushiro-Dori** – holds, made in the stance at attacking from behind.

Ikkajo

A base for mastering all technical actions of Daito-ryu Aikijujutsu is thirty holds of Ikkajo, which high-quality mastering allows to oppose practically all types of attacks from four world sides. It is necessary to say that all, who practice Aikido, must not mistake the term Ikkajo (first control) – technical hold of this martial art for Ikkajo (first group) in Daito-ryu. Ikkajo in Aikido is an analogue of only the first hold (Ippondori) of thirty absolutely different techniques of Daito-ryu Aikijujutsu.

Ikkajo Tachiai

Ippondori

The first variant: *Ippon Dori Omote*
(fig.26-37)

The attacking person (Uke) makes the step forward by the right leg from the left-side stance and strikes Shomen Uchi on the left shoulder or head of the defending person (Tori). If to allow the adversary to conduct the blow to the last phase, its blocking is practically impossible, because the energy, inset in the attacking extremity's effort reaches its maximum, and it is necessary to apply more force and energy to resist it. Another conception is realized in Daito-ryu Aikijujutsu. The blocking effect must be realized at the moment of the adversary's swing, when his body is not steady and at such an angle to take Uke out of balance.

At Uke's swing moment, Tori makes the step by the left leg forward and blocks the attacking extremity, putting the left arm on the striking one near the shoulder, and presses forward and a bit to the right. Tori strikes the direct blow in adversary's ribs by the right fist, after that he catches the arm of the attacking person near the wrist. Tori moves his right leg forward, turns his hips to the right and presses Uke's shoulder by the left palm down, laying him on the ground. The attacking person strikes the kick by the left leg in adversary's ribs from aside, after that place the shin near his right armpit. Tori moves his body down, places the adversary's caught extremity on the right hip and presses it by his whole body. It allows him to lower the opponent's arm by his left one, keeping the pain holding. He makes the swing up by the left arm and strikes Shomen Uchi on Uke's neck.

After that it is necessary to make the step back by the left leg, at that the right arm must continue to control the opponent's arm, and the look must trace all his actions.

Tori releases the hold and takes the initial position. His look controls all adversary's movements as before.

Uke stands up and returns to the initial position, also without taking his look away from Tori's face. The bow.

Second variant: *Ippon Dori Ura*
(fig.38-49)

The attacking person makes the step forward by the right leg from the left-side stance and strikes Shomen Uchi by the right palm rib on the head or collar bone of the attacking person.

Tori makes the step forward by the left leg and blocks this attack at the swing moment. At that his left palm is near the adversary's right elbow, and the right one near his wrist. The right hand of the defending person catches the hand of the attacking one and pulls it back and down. Synchronously with it Tori pushes Uke's elbow up by the right arm.

Tori turns by 180 degrees to the right, taking the right leg on arc back. Synchronously with it he presses Uke's elbow by the left palm, forcing him to lay on the ground face down.

The defending person lowers on the knees, placing his left knee near the opponent's right armpit. He presses Uke's right arm to the ground by his arms. Keeping the grip by the right arm, Tori strikes the finishing Shomen Uchi by the left palm rib in the adversary's neck.

After that Tori turns on the knees by 90 degrees to the left without taking his look away from the opponent and stands in the stance.

Uke also stands up in the stance. Both return to the initial position. The bow.

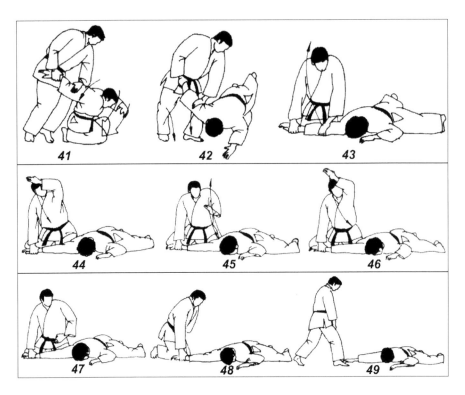

Kuruma Daoshi
(fig.50-58)

The attacking person makes the step forward by the right leg from the right-side stance and strikes Yokomen Uchi in the temple or neck of the defending person. Tori makes the step by the left leg forward and bocks the attack by the left forearm. The blocking must be attended by taking Uke out of balance. For that the effort of the blocking arm must be directed forward and to the left, turning the opponent to the same side.

After that Tori steps by the right leg behind the adversary's left lead one and strikes the blow by the right palm in the head, or pushes Uke's left shoulder, overturning him on the ground. Synchronously with the push by the arm, the torso turns to the left. The impact on the opponent must be realized by the arc trajectory from the right to the left and top-down.

Tori moves his left leg to Uke's torso, at that keeping his right arm by the left one, after which strikes Chomen Uchi on the throat. Then Tori releases his grip and straightens his torso. Uke stands in the stance. Both return to the initial position. The bow.

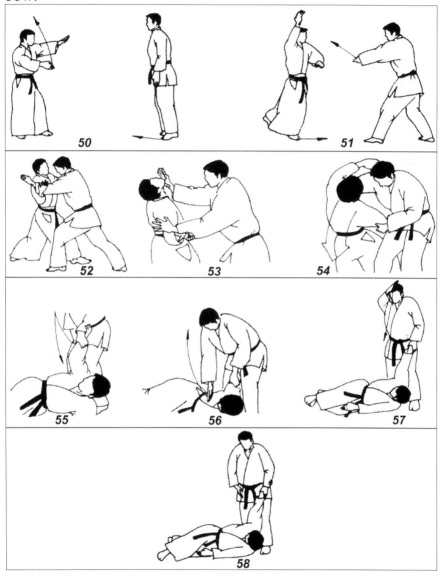

Gyaku Ude-dori
(fig.59-79)

The attacking person makes the step forward by the right leg from the readiness position and catches the cloth of the defending person by the lapel by the right hand.

Working for advance, Tori makes the step forward to the right by the right leg and turns the torso to the left, before Uke doesn't fix his grip and doesn't continue the started combination. Synchronously with it he squeezes his hands in fists, moves them up and strikes the ascending blow by the right fist from the thumb side in the chin, and on the adversary's attacking arm near the elbow by the left fist.

Continuing to move his extremities, Tori makes the swing up, synchronously striking the kick by the left knee in the opponent's belly. After that he moves his fists down and strikes the blow in the bridge by the right fist rib, and in the elbow joint of the attacking person's right arm – by the left one, in such a way weakening his grip.

After that, Tori catches Uke's hand by his right one and the elbow by his left palm. He breaks the grip by the fast movement, twists the adversary's hand clockwise, moves the left hand on arc up forward, to the right down, and lowers him down on the ground, pressing the elbow by the left arm.

Keeping control over Uke's arm and pushing him forward, Tori makes the step by the left leg diagonally to the left, striking the blow on his torso, and lays the opponent face down. Having fixed Uke's hand on his right hip, Tori releases the grip by the left arm and strikes the descending Shomen Uchi by the palm rib on his neck.

Tori steps back by the left leg. He breaks the grip and puts the right leg to the left one, continuing to fix all Uke's movements by the look. Uke takes the stance. Both return to the initial position. The bow.

Koshi Guruma
(fig.80-93)

The attacking person comes close to the defending one from the readiness position, makes the step forward by the left leg and catches his cloth by the lapel by both hands.

Tori makes the step to the left by the right leg and strikes the ascending blow in the opponent's belly by both fists.

After that, Tori moves his right hand up from the external side and catches Uke's elbow bend by it. Synchronously with it he catches the right elbow of the attacking person from below by his left hand.

Tori makes the step back to the right by the right leg. Synchronously with it he pulls the adversary's left arm down by his right hand, and pushes Uke's right arm up by his left one. Thus Uke is out of balance.

Tori makes the step by the left leg to the right and puts his left hip forward. After that, he throws his opponent on the ground.

Tori keeps the opponent's arm by his left one and strikes Shomen Uchi in the throat by the rib of his right one.

Tori releases the grip, makes the step by the left leg back and straightens. Uke takes the stance. Both return to the initial position. The bow.

80

81

82

83

84

85

86

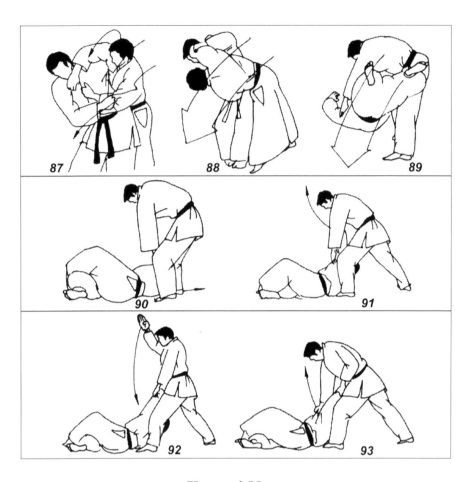

Karami Nage
(fig.94-114)

Uke comes close to Tori from the initial position, makes the step by the left leg forward and catches his cloth near the right shoulder by the left hand. After that, he raises the right arm up and strikes Shomen Uchi on the head or shoulder of the defending person.

As we can see from the situation, the time for realizing the earlier trained hold Gyaku Ude-dori is lost, because Uke has already begun to continue his attack after catching Tori's cloth. Tori makes the step forward by the right leg. He raises both arms up, in such a way that the right one passes from the external side from Uke's left one, and the left arm – from the external side, and blocks the attack. The defending person's left palm is on the attacking person's right elbow joint, and his right palm – near his wrist.

Moving the attacking person's caught right arm on arc to the right down, Tori crosses the adversary's extremities.

After that, Tori moves the right hand back to the hip, squeezes the fist and strikes the blow in opponent's floating ribs.

The defending person catches the adversary's left arm near the wrist, breaks the grip and moves it on arc up, synchronously with it he moves the opponent's right arm on arc down, in such a way making the cross lock.

Tori makes the step forward to the right by the left leg and puts it in front of the adversary's left lead leg and throws Uke on the ground, continuing to apply efforts to the cross lock.

Tori makes the step back by the right leg and pulls Uke's crossed arms on him and down till his right hand touches the ground and he is turned face down. In this position Uke cannot conduct the counterattack by the kick.

After that, Tori stands on the knees in such a way that his left knee is leant against the adversary's right armpit. He continues to make the exercise by the left arm, and strikes Shomen Uchi on the opponent's neck by the right palm rib.

Tori, then Uke take the stance and return to the initial position. The bow.

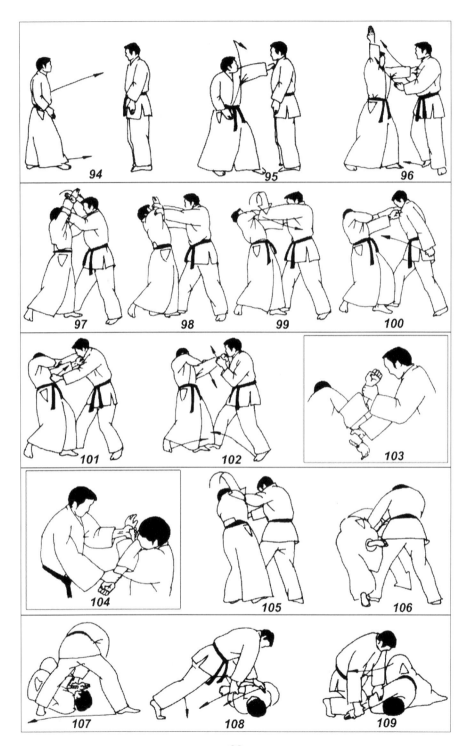

94　　　　　95　　　　　96

97　　　　98　　　　99　　　　100

101　　　　102　　　　103

104　　　　105　　　　106

107　　　　108　　　　109

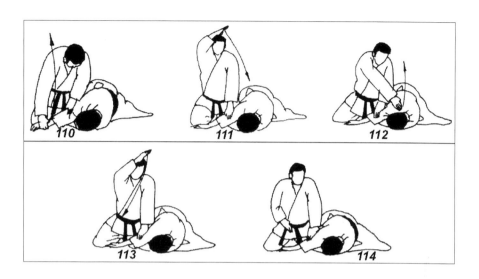

Ura Otoshi
(fig.115-120)

Uke comes close to Tori from the initial position, makes the step forward by the right leg and catches the left sleeve near the elbow joint by the right hand.

At the moment, when the defending person makes the step forward by the right leg and only begins to catch the cloth, he is in the best position for being taken out of balance. Tori makes the big step by the left leg forward towards the attack and a bit to the left, bends the elbow and catches the adversary's left elbow. Tori's body moves forward, so Uke loses balance and bends back to the right.

Using it, Tori makes the big step forward by the right leg and raises the extended right arm up, in such a way pressing the adversary's extremity bottom-up. Immediately after that, Tori bends his torso down and forward, overturning the opponent on the ground.

Continuing to keep the adversary's right arm by the left one, Tori makes the swing by the right arm and strikes Shomen Uchi on Uke's throat. Tori releases the grip, makes the step back by the right leg, puts the left one close to it and straightens.

Uke lifts from the ground. Both return to the initial position. The bow.

Obi Otoshi
(fig.121-129)

Uke comes close to Tori from the initial position, makes the step forward by the right leg and catches the cloth lapel by both hands for making a throw through the hip or a forward trip.

Tori makes the step to the left by the right leg and turns the torso to the right. Synchronously with it he strikes the blow by both fists in the opponent's belly.

After that, he makes the big step forward by the left leg. He moves the left arm between Uke's ones and catches his throat. He catches the adversary's belt by the right hand.

After that, he fixes the low part of the attacking person's body by the right arm, and moves the left arm at first up forward, in such a way taking Uke out of balance and putting him on the tiptoes, then abruptly down, overturning the adversary on the ground.

After that, Tori strikes Shomen Uchi on the throat by the right palm rib.

Tori makes the step back by the left leg, puts the right leg close to it and takes the initial waiting stance.

Uke lifts from the ground. Both return to the initial position. The bow.

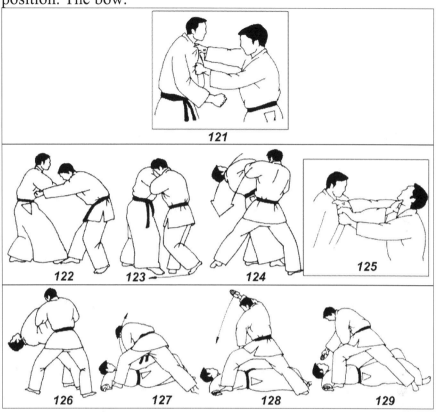

Kiri Gaeshi
(fig.130-143)

Uke comes close to Tori from the initial position, makes the step forward by the right leg and catches both his arms near the elbow bend by his hands. The defending person makes the little step to the left by the right leg, turns his torso to the left and moves both arms on arc in the same direction and a bit up.

After that Tori makes the step by the right leg to the right, turns the torso in the same direction and raises both arms to the right and up. His right arm is placed near the forehead.

The defending person makes the step by the left leg forward behind the adversary's lead leg. Synchronously with it he extends the left arm forward and presses it to the opponent's breast.

Turning the torso to the left by the abrupt movement and pushing the left arm in the same direction, Tori throws Uke over the left leg, put forward, on the ground.

Tori turns by 180 degrees to the left and makes the step back by the left leg. He strikes Shomen Uchi on the adversary's throat by the right palm rib.

Tori puts the right leg to the left one and takes the waiting stance. Uke lifts from the ground. Both return to the initial position. The bow.

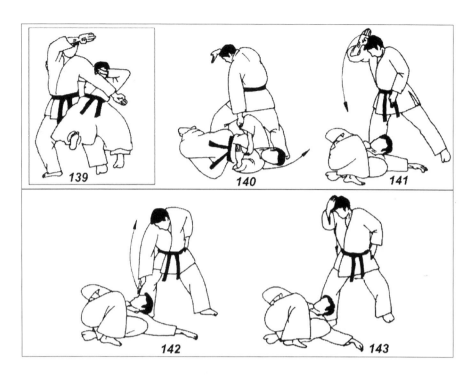

Kote Gaeshi
(fig.144-162)

Uke comes close to Tori from the initial position, makes the step forward by the right leg and catches his arms near the wrists by own hands.

Tori straightens his arms, extending them down and forward.

After that the defending person claps by palms of the caught hands in front of him at the belly level. Then he raises the forearms of the arms, bent in the elbows, vertically up. At this position the movement force is directed against both Uke's thumbs that makes his grip very weak.

Tori catches Uke's left thumb by the right hand and break the grip, twisting it counterclockwise.

After that the defending person lays his left arm on the twisted opponent's hand from above and overturns the adversary on the ground, intensifying the impact on it.

The adversary is lying on the spine. Tori lowers on his knees, pulls Uke's caught hand on him and places it between his legs. After that, he places his left palm on the adversary's elbow and keeps him immovable by pressing it.

Tori strikes Shomen Uchi on the opponent's throat by the right palm rib. Tori lifts from the knees and takes the waiting stance. Uke lifts from the ground. Both return to the initial position. The bow.

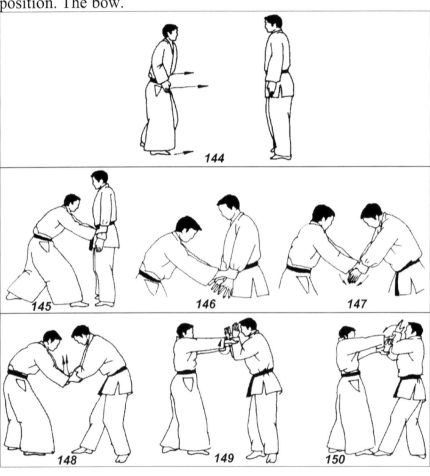

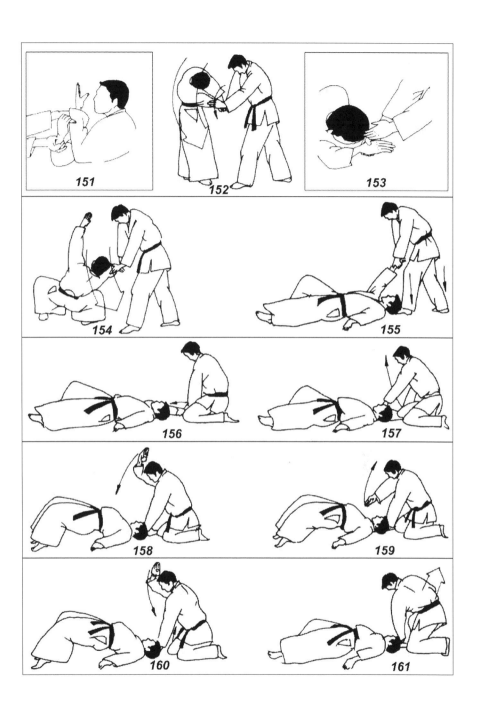

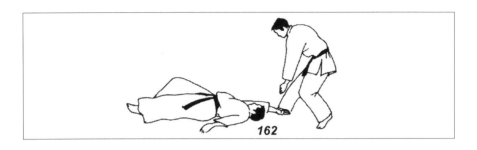

162

Shiho Nage
Variant #1 (fig.163-167)

Uke comes close to Tori from the initial position, makes the step forward by the right leg and tries to catch the adversary's left arm near the wrist by the homonymous hand.

Tori follows the attacking person's movement and begins to move the left arm towards the applied adversary's force, not allowing him to fix his grip. The torso turns to the right, the right leg makes the step on arc back.

The attacking person's grip is weakened, because Tori's attacked extremity begins to move before Uke stops trying to squeeze the hand. At the same time the movement of the defending person's caught arm is made towards Uke's right thumb that makes the try to conduct the grip impossible.

Tori catches the opponent's arm by the right hand and turns clockwise back, shifting his body gravity center.

Tori's right hand catches Uke's wrist in such a way that his thumb presses the point, where pulse is felt.

Without taking the feet position, Tori fast turns by 180 degrees and raises his hands above the head. The arms must not be bent in the elbows, and the movement itself reminds of a swing by a sword above the head.

Having finished the body turn, Tori lowers his arms down, moves his body forward down and overturns the opponent on the ground.

Tori puts the right leg to the left one and takes the readiness position. Uke lifts from the ground. Both return to the initial position. The bow.

163   164   165

166   167

Shiho Nage
Variant #2 (fig.168-177)

Uke comes close to Tori, makes the step forward by the right leg, catching his arms by own hands.

At the moment when the attacking person tries to fix his grip, the defending one makes the step by the left leg forward. The elbows remain immovable, and forearms move a bit forward and up. The thumbs of the caught extremities are directed up. Uke's grip becomes very weak in this position.

Tori catches Uke's right arm by his right hand.

Tori turns by 180 degrees to the right and raise his arms, unbent in the elbows, over his head.

Having finished the body turn, Tori lowers his arms down, moves his body forward down and overturns the adversary on the ground.

The adversary is lying on his spine. It is necessary to trace that his caught arm remains bent in the elbow. Tori catches his elbow by the left palm, presses it down and makes the pain holding.

Tori strikes Shomen Uchi on the adversary's throat by the right palm rib.

Tori lifts from his knees and steps a bit back. Uke lifts from the ground. Both return to the initial position. The bow.

Ikkajo Idori

Ippon Dori
Variant Omote (fig.178-191)

The initial position: both adversaries are in front of each other on the knees.

Uke puts his left foot on the ground, the right knee remains on the floor, the arms take the martial position.

Uke's left knee lowers on the ground, the right leg makes the step forward and is put on the foot. Synchronously with it he makes the swing by the right arm for the further chopping Shomen Uchi by the palm rib on Tori's head or shoulder.

At the swing moment, when the attacking person is in the weakest position, the defending one makes the step forward by the left leg and blocks the adversary's attacking extremity by his arms. At that Tori's left arm is on Uke's right elbow, and the right one – on his forearm near the wrist. At blocking the defending person's arms are straightened, the body moves forward, at which expanse the attacking person loses balance.

Tori strikes the direct blow by opponent's ribs by the right fist, at that his left arm continues to control Uke's elbow.

The defending person's right hand catches the adversary's right forearm. The right leg makes the step forward to the right. The arms press down, making the lever of the elbow down, and Tori lays Uke on the ground face down.

Tori's torso turns to the right, the right leg lowers on the ground, the left knee is taken near Uke's right armpit.

Tori continues to keep the opponent's caught extremity by the right hand and strikes the chopping Shomen Uchi on his neck by the left palm rib.

After that, Tori releases the grip and lowers his arms on the hips.

Uke lifts from the ground in the knee stance. Moving on the knees, both return to the initial point. The bow.

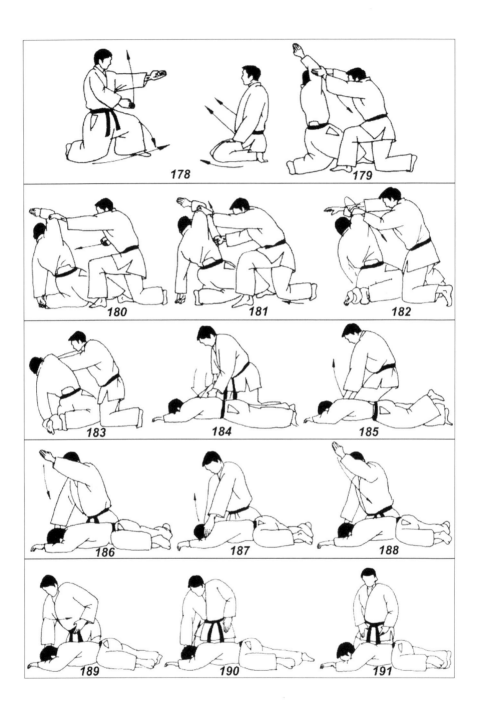

Ippon Dori
Variant Ura (fig.192-203)

Uke takes the martial stance on the right knee from the initial position, then the makes the step forward by the right leg, lowering the left knee down. Synchronously with it he strikes Shomen Uchi on Tori's head or shoulder.

Tori moves forward on the knees and blocks this attack by his arms. The defending person's left palm is on the elbow of the attacking arm, and the right palm catches the forearm near the wrist.

Tori's torso turns to the right, the right leg is taken on arc to the right. Tori makes the lever of Uke's elbow down, moves him on arc around himself and lays on the ground face down. The defending person presses the adversary's caught arm to the ground, places the left knee besides Uke's right armpit, in such a way making the pain holding.

Keeping the opponent's caught extremity by the right arm Tori makes the swing by the left one and strikes Shomen Uchi on his neck by the palm rib.

Tori takes the waiting positions on the knees. Uke lifts from the ground in the knee stance. Moving on the knees, both return to the initial point. The bow.

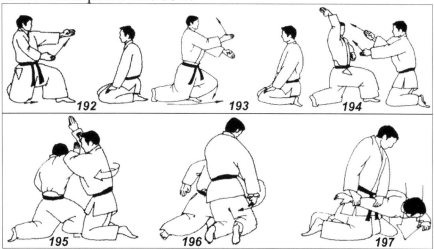

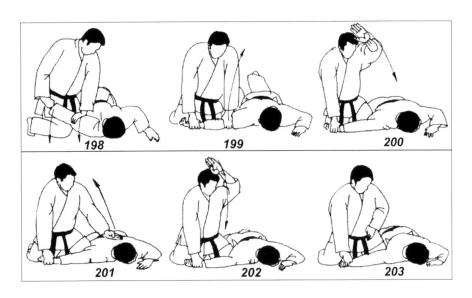

198   199   200

201   202   203

Gyaku Ude-dori
(fig.204-219)

Uke comes close to Tori (on the knees) from the initial position and catches his jacket lapel by the right hand, trying then to strike the blow by the by the free left arm.

Tori turns his torso to the left fast and strikes the ascending blow by the left fist from the thumb side in the zone of the adversary's left elbow, and the ascending one from the thumb side in the chin from below - by the right fist.

Tori's arms move up for a swing and immediately strike the descending blow by the right fist rib on the opponent's bridge, and in his elbow bend – by the left palm rib.

Tori catches Uke's right elbow by the left hand, and his hand - by the right one and steps by the right leg forward.

The defending person twists the adversary's hand by the right one, in such a way breaking the grip. Synchronously with it he rotates the opponent's arm on arc up to the right down, synchronously makes the lever of the elbow down and the bend of the hand inside, laying Uke on the ground face down.

Tori presses Uke's caught arm to the ground and makes the pain holding. It is necessary to trace that the caught arm must be at the level of Uke's shoulder, perpendicularly to his body. Tori's left knee is pressed to the adversary's right armpit. The defending person keeps the arm of the attacking one in the pain holding by his right arm and strikes Shomen Uchi on his neck by the left arm rib. Tori releases the grip and takes the waiting knee position. Uke lifts from the ground and takes the analogous position. Moving on the knees, both return to the initial point. The bow.

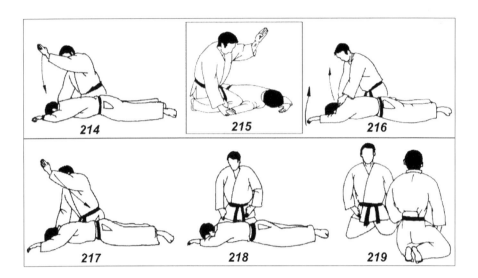

214   215   216

217   218   219

Hiji Gaeshi
(fig.220-228)

Uke comes close to Tori from the initial position and catches his cloth on the breast.

The defending person catches the adversary's attacking hand and presses it to the own body.

Synchronously with it he puts his left leg on the foot, and strikes the blow by the right fist in the adversary's belly or solar plexus.

Tori takes his right arm behind the opponent's right elbow from below and as if moves it round bottom-up by the rubbing movement. At that if Uke doesn't bend his elbow his arm will be in the elbow pain lever position. Uke's elbow bends.

At this moment Tori turns by 180 degrees to the right and takes the position on the left knee. Synchronously with it his right arm moves following the torso turn on arc up to the right down and forward. Thus, Tori twists the adversary's elbow and throws him on the ground.

At once when Uke is lying on the spine, Tori strikes the finishing Shomen Uchi by the right palm rib on the adversary's neck or throat.

Tori takes the waiting knee position. Uke lifts from the ground and takes the analogous position. Moving on the knees, both return to the initial point. The bow.

Kuruma Daoshi
(fig.229-238)

Uke puts his left leg on the foot from the initial position on the knees and raises the arms in the martial position. Lowering the left leg on the ground and making the step by the right leg, he shortens the distance and strikes the side Yokomen Uchi by the right palm rib in the defending person's neck.

Tori makes the step forward by the left leg and lowers it on the foot, the right knee remains on the ground.

At the moment, when the adversary's right arm has passed a half of its way, he finds himself in the most vulnerable and unsteady position. Just now Tori is making his block by the left arm. At the blocking moment the defending person's arm must be straightened. Blocking is realized with pushing forward and to the left in such a way that the opponent loses balance. For intensifying this effect, Tori strikes the blow in the adversary's face or neck from the right by the right arm.

After that, the defending person catches Uke's left forearm near the wrist by left hand, and his shoulder – by the right one. He turns to the left. He pulls on himself to the left and down by the left arm and pushes from himself down by the right one, in such a way overturning Uke on the ground.

Having fixed the adversary's right arm on the ground, Tori strikes the finishing Shomen Uchi on the throat by the right palm rib.

Tori releases the grip and takes the waiting knee position. Uke lifts from the ground and takes the analogous position. Moving on the knees, both return to the initial point. The bow.

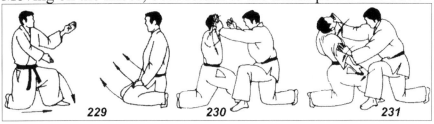

229   230   231

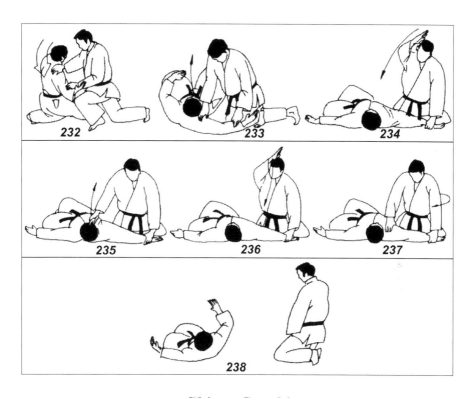

Shime Gaeshi
(fig.239-246)

Uke comes close to Tori from the initial position on the knees and grips the cloth lapel for the further throw over the spine from the knees or forward trip from a knee.

Tori strikes the blow by both fists in the adversary's belly or solar plexus, after that, he catches his left elbow bend from above by the right hand, and the right elbow – by the left hand from below.

Tori turns by 180 degrees to the right, moving the right leg on arc to the right and back. Synchronously with it he pulls the opponent's caught arm on arc down to the left, and pushes the adversary's right elbow up to the right and down by his left arm.

Uke loses balance and falls on the ground face up.

Tori keeps the opponent's arm by his left one, and strikes the finishing Shomen Uchi on his throat by his right palm rib. Tori releases the grip and takes the waiting knee position. Uke lifts from the ground and takes the analogous position. Moving on the knees, both return to the initial point. The bow.

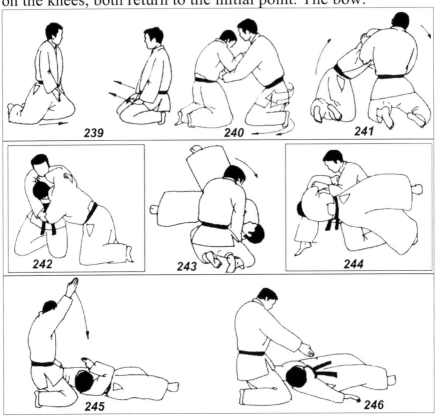

Daki Jime
(fig.247-255)

Uke comes close to Tori from the initial position on the knees and grips the cloth lapel for the further throw over the spine from the knees or forward trip from a knee.

Tori strikes the blow by both fists in the adversary's belly or solar plexus.

After that the defending person places his left forearm on the attacking person's left elbow bend, presses down and on himself and presses his forearm to the own body. Synchronously with it Tori moves his right arm from below under Uke's left one, lays the right hand on the left one, intensifying the grip in such a way.

Immediately after that, the defending person turns by 90 degrees to the right and takes the stance on one knee.

Uke's forearm is densely pressed to Tori's trunk, so he begins to feel the strong pain that forces him to fall on the ground.

For intensifying the effect from the throw, Tori makes the push by the left elbow and shoulder on Uke's body towards his effort.

The defending person lowers his right leg on the knee, controls the adversary's extremity by the left arm, and strikes the chopping Shomen Uchi by the right palm rib on his throat or neck.

Tori releases the grip and takes the waiting knee position. Uke lifts from the ground and takes the analogous position. Moving on the knees, both return to the initial point. The bow.

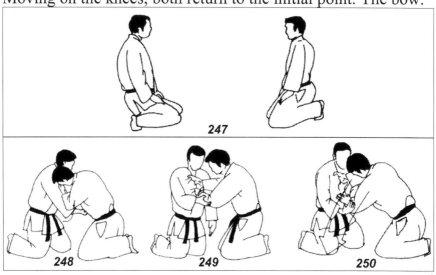

247

248   249   250

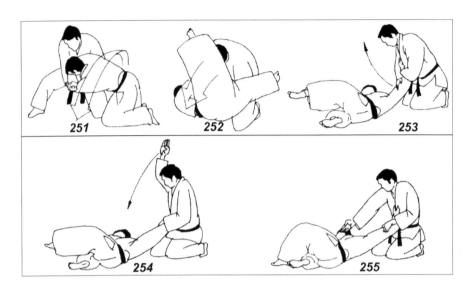

251   252   253

254   255

Karami Nage
(fig.256-270)

Uke comes close to Tori from the initial knee position and catches the cloth on his shoulder by the left hand.

Immediately after that he strikes the chopping Shomen Uchi on the adversary's head or shoulder by the right palm rib.

Tori moves forward. He raises both arms up, in such a way that the right one passes from the external side of Uke's left one, and the left one – from the internal side, and blocks the attack. The defending person's right palm is placed on the attacking person's right elbow joint, and the right palm – near his wrist.

Moving the attacking person's right arm on arc to the right and down, Tori crosses two adversary's extremities.

After that, Tori takes the right hand back to the hip, squeezes it in the fist and strikes the blow in opponent's floating ribs.

The defending person catches the adversary's left arm near the wrist, breaks the grip and moves it on arc up, synchronously with it he moves the opponent's right arm on arc down, making the cross lock in such a way.

Uke is overturned on the ground as a result of the strong pain effect.

Tori turns by 90 degrees to the right and moves his right leg on arc back. Synchronously with it he pulls Uke's crossed arms on himself, keeping them in such a way that the adversary can't move because of the strong pain in the elbow and hand.

Keeping the opponent in such position by the left arm, Tori strikes the finishing Shomen Uchi on his neck by the right palm rib. Tori releases the grip and takes the waiting position on the knees. Uke lifts from the ground and takes the analogous position. Moving on the knees, both return to the initial point. The bow.

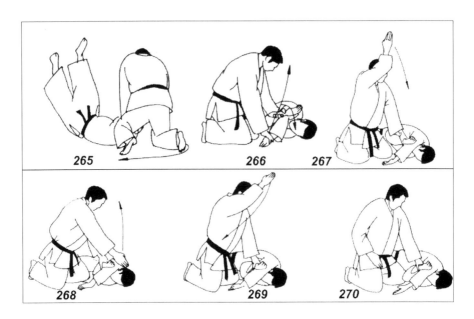

265   266   267

268   269   270

Kote Gaeshi
(fig.271-286)

Uke comes close to Tori from the initial knee position and catches his forearms near the wrists by both hands.

Tori straightens his arms, extending them down and forward.

After that the defending person claps by caught palms in front of himself at the belly level. Then he raises the forearms of the arms, bent in the elbows, vertically up. At such position the movement force is directed against Uke's thumbs that makes his grip very weak.

Tori catches Uke's left thumb by his right hand, twists it counterclockwise and breaks the grip.

After that the defending person lays his left arm on the opponent's twisted hand from above, intensifies the impact on it and overturns the adversary on the ground.

The adversary is lying on the spine. Tori lowers, pulls Uke's caught hand on himself and places it between his legs. After that he places the own left palm on his elbow, presses on it and keeps the adversary immovable.

Tori strikes Shomen Uchi on the opponent's throat by the right palm rib.

Tori releases the grip and takes the waiting position on the knees. Uke lifts from the ground and takes the analogous position. Moving on the knees, both return to the initial point. The bow.

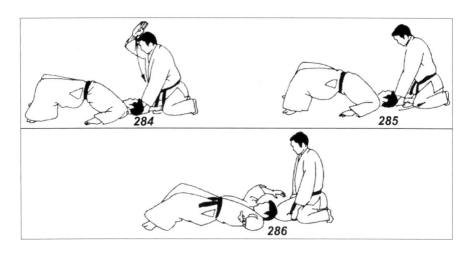

284 285 286

Nukite Dori
(fig.287-295)

Uke comes close to Tori from the initial knee position and catches his arms near the wrists by the own hands. At the moment, when the adversary becomes to make the grip, Tori moves the straightened left arm to the left and takes the opponent out of balance.

Synchronously with it Tori bends the right elbow and moves the forearm to the left towards Uke's thumb. It allows to release the arm from the grip. He strikes the chopping blow on the adversary's neck by the right palm rib.

After that, Tori moves the caught left arm on arc to the left and up. In this position he catches the attacking person's hand by his right one and twists it clockwise. He places the left palm on the adversary's left elbow, synchronously affects the hand and elbow and lays Uke on the ground.

Tori fixes Uke's hand between his knees, keeps the elbow by the left arm and strikes the chopping Shomen Uchi on his neck by the right one.

Tori releases the grip and takes the waiting position on the knees. Uke lifts from the ground and takes the analogous position. Moving on the knees, both return to the initial point. The bow.

287 288 289 290 291 292 293 294 295

Hiza Jime
(fig.296-303)

Uke comes close to Tori from the initial knee position and catches his arms near the wrists by the own hands.

At the moment, when Uke bends and catches the wrists, he is in the weakest position. At this moment Tori makes the step by the left leg back, then substeps to it by the right one.

At this moment Tori moves his arms on arc to the external sides up, inside, catches his hands and twists them in such a way that they touch each other by their back sides, and thumbs are directed down.

The defending person pulls the adversary's arms on himself, places them between his knees and strongly presses to each other, in such a way releasing his arms for the next blow.

Tori strikes the blow on the adversary's shoulders by both palm ribs.

Tori releases the grip and takes the waiting position on the knees. Uke lifts from the ground and takes the analogous position. Moving on the knees, both return to the initial point. The bow.

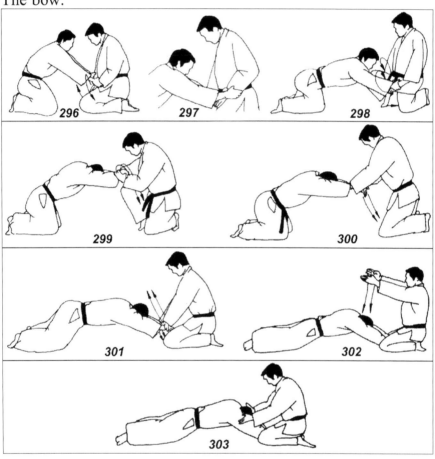

Ikkajo Hanza-Handachi

Hanmi Nage
(fig.304-312)

Initial position: Tori is in the seating knee position, Uke stands from the right of him.

The attacking person comes from aside, bends and catches Tori's right arm by his left hand.

The defending person turns the torso to the right, catches the attacking forearm near the wrist by the left hand. After that he comes close to the opponent from the right leg and raises his caught hand up at the head level, fingers are directed up, the thumb – on his forehead. The left arm continues to fix the adversary's forearm, in such a way creating the strong pain effect in his hand.

Tori turns by 180 degrees to the left and carries Uke's arm under the head, after that he leans it against the forearm of the caught arm.

After that Tori bends forward, continues to affect the attacking person's hand and throws him on the ground to the left side.

Ura Otoshi
(fig.313-320)

Initial position: Tori is in the seating knee position, Uke stands from the right of him.

The attacking person makes the step by the right leg and catches the defending person's left hand by the right one.

Tori at first moves his hand forward up, fingers are directed on the adversary. Thus he causes strong pain feelings in Uke's hand, takes him out of balance and forces to rise on the tiptoes.

Immediately after that the defending person moves his caught arm back to the left and down. His torso turns to the left, and the left leg is put on the foot.

Synchronously with it Tori beats under Uke's rear right popliteal bend by his left arm and overturns the adversary on the ground to the right from himself.

Izori
(fig.321-328)

Initial position: Tori is in the seating knee position, Uke stands from the right of him in the stance.

The attacking person comes close to Tori, makes the step by the right leg forward and catches his arms by both hands.

The defending person moves his hands forward, fingers are directed up, and in such a way he causes the pain feeling in Uke's hand, forcing him to lose balance and to rise on the tiptoes.

After that, Tori moves the arms by the sides back, bends his head and overturns the adversary over himself back.

Kata Otoshi
(fig.329-336)

Initial position: Tori is in the seating knee position, Uke stands from the right of him in the stance.

The attacking person comes close to the defending one and seizes him from behind.

Tori catches Uke's right arm in such a way that his left hand keeps the adversary's right forearm near the wrist, and the left one, raised up, keeps his arm on the shoulder.

After that Tori bends forward, puts the left leg on the foot and throws the adversary over the spine, gripping the arm on the shoulder.

Shiho Nage
(fig.337-349)

Initial position: Tori is in the seating knee position, Uke stands from the right of him in the stance.

The attacking person makes the step forward by the right leg, bends and catches the defending person's arms near the wrists by both hands.

Tori moves his hands forward up in such a way that his fingers are directed up, causing the strong pain feeling in the adversary's hands.

After that he makes the step by the right leg forward, rises and makes the step by the left leg forward. Synchronously with it he catches the opponent's right wrist by the right hand. Then he turns by 180 degrees, moves the adversary's arms over the head and makes Shiho Nage, lowering on the knee.

After that Tori makes the pain holding of Uke, affecting his bent elbow by the left palm, and strikes the finishing Shomen Uchi on the adversary's throat by the right palm rib. Tori releases the grip and takes the waiting position on the knees. Uke lifts from the ground and takes the analogous position. The bow.

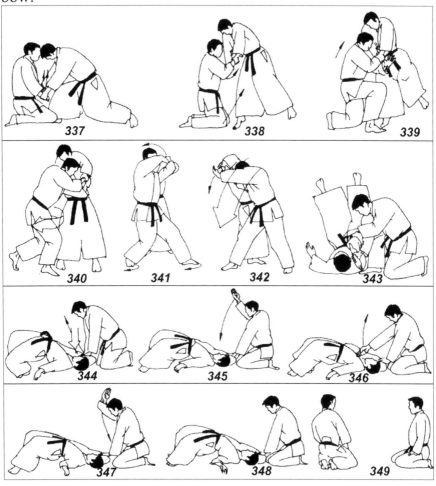

Ikkajo Ushiro-Dori

Tate Eridori
(fig.350-359)

Initial position: Both are in front of each other in the waiting position. Tori turns his spine to Uke.

Uke comes close to the adversary, makes the step forward by the right leg and catches Tori's collar from behind by the homonymous hand.

The defending person raises the right leg, bent in the knee, up and turns by 180 degrees to the left around his axis, using the left foot as a rotation center, after that he lowers the right leg on the ground.

Synchronously with putting the right leg, Tori strikes the blow by the back side of the left fist in the opponent's belly or solar plexus. Then he dives his head under Uke's right arm, after that catches his hand by his right one. The grip is realized in such a way that the thumb is approximately in the middle of the back side of the adversary's hand, rest fingers seize the palm rib densely.

Tori raises his left arm and places it on the adversary's elbow. After that, the defending person breaks the adversary's grip by the abrupt movement of both arms. This movement must be accompanied by twisting the hand to the internal side and a little push of his elbow up.

Tori continues to affect the adversary's hand by the right arm, he presses down by the left palm and lays him on the ground face down.

Tori makes the step by the left leg forward to Uke's right armpit, places his arm in the vertical plane and keeps the adversary lying prone on the ground, pressing by the right arm down on his hand.

Tori strikes the chopping Shomen Uchi on Uke's neck by the left palm rib. Tori releases the grip and takes the waiting position on the knees. Uke lifts from the ground and takes the analogous position. Both return to the initial point. The bow.

Ryo Kata Hineri
(fig.360-369)

Initial position: Both are in front of each other in the waiting position. Tori turns his spine to Uke.

The attacking person comes close to the defending one, makes the step forward by the right leg and catches his cloth on the shoulders by both hands.

Tori makes the swing by the left arm, raises the left leg, bent in the knee, up and turns around the own axis by 180 degrees to the right, using the right foot as a rotation point.

After that, Tori lowers his left leg on the ground, putting it behind the adversary's lead leg. Synchronously with it he dives his head under the opponent's left arm, extends his left arm forward to the left and places it near his breast.

The defending person pushes his adversary by the left arm back in the breast, raises his right leg by the right hand and throws him over the left leg, put forward, on the ground.

Tori turns by 180 degrees to the left, makes the step back by the left leg and strikes the finishing Shomen Uchi by the right palm rib in the adversary's neck.

Tori puts the right leg to the left one and takes the waiting position. Uke lifts from the ground and takes the analogous position. Both return to the initial positon. The bow.

360

Ryo Hiji Gaeshi
(fig.370-377)

Initial position: Both are in front of each other in the waiting position. Tori turns his spine to Uke.

The attacking person comes close to the defending one and catches his elbows from behind by the own hands.

Tori extends his arms, straightened in the elbows, forward up. Synchronously with it he bends and moves his pelvis strongly back and up, in such a way raising Uke, and forces him to rise on the tiptoes and to lose balance.

After that, Tori makes the step by the right leg back behind the adversary's legs. He turns approximately by 90 degrees to the right. He places his forearms near the opponent's torso, and takes the left arm to the left leg.

Tori bends back and throws the adversary over his right leg, pushing him by the right arm in the movement direction. Tori helps the throw by the left hand, raising Uke's left leg.

After that, Tori turns approximately by 90 degrees to the right. He substeps by the left leg a bit to the left and strikes the chopping blow by the right palm rib in the adversary's neck.

Tori puts the right leg to the left one and takes the waiting position. Uke lifts from the ground and takes the analogous position. Both return to the initial position. The bow.

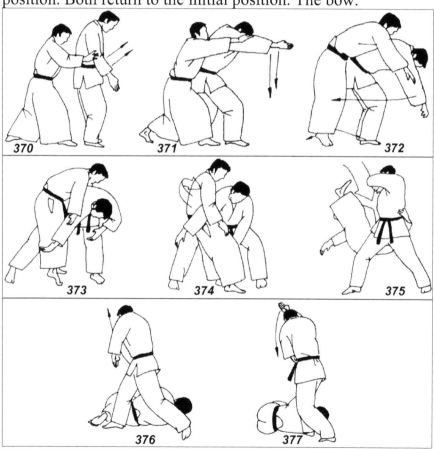

Daki Jime Dori
(fig.378-388)

Initial position: Both are in front of each other in the waiting position. Tori turns his spine to Uke.

The Uke comes close to the defending person and seizes his trunk under the arms from behind.

Tori strikes the blow on the back side of Uke's right hand, placed above his left hand, by phalanxes of squeezed left fingers.

After that, Tori rises the left leg, bent in the knee, and turns by 180 degrees to the right, using the right foot as a rotation axis.

Synchronously with it Tori catches the adversary's right hand by his right one in such a way that his thumb is placed on the back side of the right hand and rest fingers seize the palm rib.

Synchronously with it the defending person breaks the adversary's grip, then puts the left leg and twists it clockwise. Tori places his left arm on Uke's right elbow, presses on it and lays the opponent on the ground face down.

Tori puts his left leg to the opponent's right armpit and makes the pain holding of his right leg.

After that, Tori strikes the chopping blow by the right palm rib in the adversary's neck.

Tori releases the grip and takes the waiting position. Uke lifts from the ground and takes the analogous position. Both return to the initial point. The bow.

378   379   380

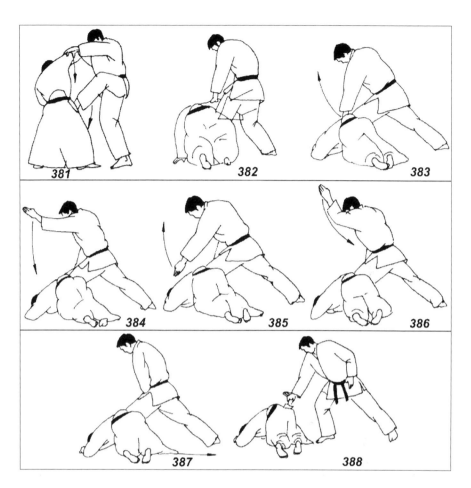

381 382 383 384 385 386 387 388

Kata Otoshi
(fig.389-399)

Initial position: Both are in front of each other in the waiting position. Tori turns his spine to Uke.

Uke comes close to Tori and seizes his trunk above the arms.

Tori makes the little step back by the right leg and raises his arms, bent in the elbows, up by the sides. They rise to the horizontal level. Thus Tori breaks the adversary's grip.

After that the defending person catches the attacking person's right forearm near the wrist by his left hand, and throws it on the shoulder by the right one.

Tori lowers on the right knee and makes the throw over the spine with the grip on the shoulder from the knee. The adversary is on the ground spine down.

Tori continues to keep the opponent's right arm by the own left arm and strikes the finishing Shomen Uchi on his throat by the right palm rib.

Tori releases the grip and takes the waiting position. Uke lifts from the ground and takes the analogous stance. Both return to the initial point. The bow.

389 390 391 392

393 394 395

396 397

398

399

Chapter 3
Selected Techniques Hiden Mokuroku

Nikajo - Gokajo

Further we'll consider the most typical selected holds of Daito-ryu Aikijujutsu, related to the section Hiden Mokuroku. Despite the fact that not all technical actions of the school are presented to readers' attention, they completely elucidate all applied aspects of this Budo type.

Nikajo
(Review of selected techniques)

Idori

Konoha Gaeshi
(fig.400-403)
Tori comes close to Uke, forestalling his attack. Synchronously with it, he strikes the direct distracting blow in the face by fingers of the right hand, forcing the opponent to bend back.

Tori catches fingers of Uke's right hand by the homonymous one and twists his hand in such a way that it turns palm forward, and his right elbow is directed up. Synchronously with it he strikes the blow in adversary's ribs by the left fist.

Tori moves his left palm to Uke's right elbow and turns to the right, continuing to affect adversary's fingers by the right arm, and forces him to move on arc down.

Tori steps on Uke's right palm by the right knee, in such a way beginning its holding, after which he strikes the finishing blow by the left palm rib.

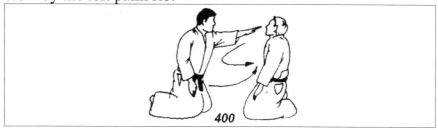

400

401   402   403

Kataha Dori
(fig.404-407)

Uke comes close to the opponent fast and strikes the direct Chudan Tsuki by the right fist in the solar plexus zone. Tori turns to the right and synchronously moves the right leg on arc back, in such a way shifting from the attack line. Synchronously with it he catches the adversary's attacking extremity near the hand by the right one, and strikes the blow on his ribs by the left fist.

Uke falls forward. Using it, Tori moves the adversary's caught extremity by himself, continuing to turn to the right. The puts the right leg on the whole foot. The left leg remains on the knee. Tori presses in the zone of the adversary's right elbow by his trunk, in such a way setting the pain control over his arm. Synchronously with it he seizes the opponent's neck for best fixing and managing it.

Tori turns to the left. He catches the left lapel of the adversary's kimono by the homonymous hand and begins to pull him back, continuing to affect his elbow by the trunk. When Uke is overturned on the ground, Tori finishes beating the adversary.

404

| 405 | 406 | 407 |

Hanza-Handachi

Suso Dori
(fig. 408 – 411)

Tori and Uke are in front of each other. Tori is seating in the knee position, Uke – standing. Uke makes the step by the right leg forward and synchronously with it strikes the chopping Shomen Uchi by the right palm rib. Tori moves forward and to the left, going away from the attack line aside. Synchronously with it he catches the adversary's lead leg from the back side of the knee and near the ankle by the own hands. After that, Tori affects the opponent's caught leg by the arms and overturns him on the ground. He steps on Uke's leg by the left knee, in such a way fixing him on the ground. After that he strikes the finishing Uraken Uchi on adversary's ribs by the left fist.

408

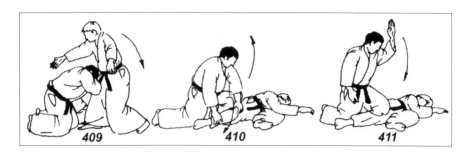

409   410   411

Tachiai

Gyaku Dasuki
(fig. 412 – 415)

Tori and Uke are in front of each other in the standing position. Uke makes the step forward by the right leg and synchronously with it strikes the chopping blow by the right palm rib. Tori makes the step forward by the left leg, coming close to the adversary. Synchronously with it, he blocks the attack by the left palm, laying it on the elbow of the adversary's attacking extremity. The strikes the direct blow in the adversary's belly or solar plexus by the right fist.

Tori fixes Uke's right shoulder by the left arm, he seizes the adversary's neck from the front by the right one. Synchronously with it he steps behind the opponent's legs by the right leg. Having linked his hands, Tori throws Uke on the tatami. Keeping the opponent on the ground, Tori strikes the finishing Empi Uchi on adversary's ribs by the right elbow.

412

413   414   415

Seikujiki
(fig.416 – 419)

Tori and Uke are in front of each other in the standing position. Uke makes the step forward by the right leg and synchronously with it catches Tori's jacket lapels by both hands by the cross grip. Tori makes the step forward by the right leg, turning the right foot to the external side. Synchronously with it he strikes the blow on adversary's ribs by both fists.

The defending person makes the big step forward behind the adversary's lead leg by the left one. He catches the adversary's belt from the front by the right hand. Synchronously with it he strikes Tegatana Uchi on Uke's neck by the left palm rib. Then Tori moves farther behind the opponent and synchronously with takes him out of balance. After that, he overturns Uke back. This action may be accompanied by beating under the adversary's knee bend. As a final, Tori strikes the chopping blows by both hands in the opponent's throat and belly.

416

417   418   419

Ushiro-Dori

Tsukitaoshi
(fig.420 – 423)

The initial position – standing, Uke is behind Tori's spine. Uke makes the step forward by the right leg and synchronously with it catches Tori's jacket lapel behind near the neck. Tori turns by 180 degrees to the right, using the right foot as a turning point. Synchronously with it he strikes the blow on adversary's ribs by the right palm rib. Then he affects the elbow bend of the opponent's right arm, bending it. He steps behind Uke's right leg by his right one. Synchronously wit it he pushes the adversary's chin by the right palm and beats under his leg by the right one, in such a way throwing Uke on the ground.

Nikajo Ura. Gyaku Dasuki
(fig.424 – 427)

Nikajo Ura – is, in fact, execution of the already studied techniques in Ura manner, that is in combination with round rotary shifts. An illustrative example may be execution of Gyaku Dasuki hold in Ura manner. In general this hold is realized in the same way that in the already studied variant with only difference that Tori is as if screwed in the hold on the round trajectory, finishing his attack by the throw over the hip.

425   426   427

Sankajo
(Review of selected techniques)

Idori

Makizume
(fig.428-431)

Tori and Uke are in front of each other in the knee stances. Uke puts the right leg forward and synchronously with it strikes the chopping descending blow by the right palm rib. Tori comes close to Uke and blocks the adversary's attack by both arms in the initial phase of the blow. At that the left hand catches the elbow of the attacking extremity, and the right one is placed on the forearm near the hand base. Tori fixes Uke's elbow by the left arm, he catches the adversary's hand by fingers by the right hand and twists the caught hand palm forward. After that, he moves the right arm a bit forward in such a way that the adversary's arm is bent with the elbow, directed up. Tori strikes the blow on opponent's ribs by the left fist. Then he catches the adversary's twisted hand from the external side by the left hand, keeping the pain effect position. After that he moves the adversary's caught extremity down. At the expanse of the pain effect, he is forced to bend. Tori strikes the chopping finishing blow on Uke's neck by the right palm rib.

428

Gasso Dori
(fig.432-435)

Tori and Uke are in front of each other in the knee stances. Forestalling Uke's attack, Tori shortens the distance and makes the false attack in front of the adversary's face by both arms, forcing him to bend back. Using the moment, Tori catches the adversary's homonymous arms near the hands by the own ones. After that he crosses Uke arms and presses them to his belly. He continues to keep the opponent's pressed arms crossed, and strikes the point Atemi in the throat by the right fist with the second phalanx, put forward.

Hanza-Handachi

Waki Dori
(fig.436-439)

The opponents are in front of each other, Tori – in the knee position, Uke –standing. Uke makes the step forward by the right leg and synchronously with it extends the homonymous arm for gripping or striking the adversary. Tori acts for advance and catches the attacking extremity near the hand base by both hands. Then he begins to turn to the right, synchronously moving the adversary's caught extremity on arc to the left up, then to the right and down. At this rotary movement Tori twists the opponent's hand and synchronously with it "outlines" Uke's caught extremity by the left forearm. In the final position Tori's both hands twist Uke's one and keep it twisted, the left forearm and elbow press on the adversary's right forearm and elbow, respectively. Because of strong pain feelings, Uke is forced to bend forward. Using it, Tori keeps Uke's caught hand by the right one, and strikes Empi Uchi on the spine by the left elbow.

Tachiai

Kubiwa
(fig.440-443)

The opponents are in front of each other in the standing position. Uke makes the step by the right leg and synchronously with it strikes the direct Chudan Tsuki by the homonymous fist in the solar plexus zone. Tori turns the torso to the right, makes the little step forward and to the left by the left leg, and the step on arc back – by the right leg, and synchronously with it, he takes the attack away from himself by the left forearm. Tori strikes the blow in the chin by the back side of the right hand, forcing the adversary to raise his head. After that he catches Uke's throat. He steps behind the opponent's lead leg, beats him under the knee and makes the back trip. The hold is finished by the descending chopping Tegatana Uchi by the left arm rib.

440

441   442   443

Ganseki Otoshi
(fig.444-447)

The opponents are in front of each other in the standing position. Uke makes the step forward by the right leg and catches Tori's heteronymous arms by both hands. The defending person keeps his arms in front of himself and turns the right foot to the external side, then makes the wide step by the left leg forward and to the right. Synchronously with it he turns by180 degrees to the right. Then he finishes the turn and makes the step back by the right leg. Synchronously with turning, he catches the adversary's right arm near its wrist by the right hand, and releases his left arm from the grip. The release is made by the movement to the opposite side from the bend of the thumb of the catching hand. Uke's arms are on Tori's left shoulder. He picks them up from below by the left arm, bends it in the elbow and fixes them in this position. Uke feels the strong pain in the elbow joints that forces him to rise on the tiptoes. Straightening the knees and a bit bending, Tori makes the thow over the shoulder.

444

445   446   447

Ushiro Dori

Kiriha
(448-451)

The initial position – standing, Uke is behind Tori's spine. Uke comes to Tori and seizes him by both arms from behind. Tori strikes the descending kick on the adversary's foot by the left leg. Then he strikes Atemi on the back sides of the opponent's arms by bent phalanxes of all fingers. He catches Uke's left arm and breaks the grip. After that, Tori turns by 180 degrees to the left, catches fingers of the opponent's left hand by the right one, and twists it. Synchronously with it he affects the adversary's elbow by the left arm and bends the arm behind the spine. The strong pain feelings in the hand and elbow force Uke to lower down on the tatami. Tori begins to hold Uke.

Yonkajo
(Review of selected techniques)

Tachiai

Uchi Gote
(fig.452-455)

The opponents are standing in front of each other. Uke makes the step forward by the right leg and synchronously strikes the descending chopping Men Uchi tangentially from the right to the left by the palm rib. Tori blocks it by the left arm. He catches the adversary's attacking extremity by both hands and moves it on arc to the left and down. Synchronously with it, he twists his wrist, makes the pinning hold of the hand and presses the point on the internal side of the adversary's wrist by the thumb. The strong pain feeling forces Uke to lower down. Tori keeps the opponent by the pain control of his arm and strikes the descending Empi Uchi by the left elbow.

452

453   454   455

Kakae Kubi
(fig.456-459)

The opponents are in front of each other in the standing positions. Uke makes the step by the right leg forward and synchronously with it catches Tori's left arm by the right hand. Tori makes the step forward by the left leg. Synchronously with it he moves the caught extremity on arc down, to the left and up. He strikes the direct blow in the solar plexus zone by the right fist.

Tori continues to move his left arm by the arc trajectory to the right and down. Thus, his hand is above the adversary's twisted right hand. In this position Uke feels the strong pain in the wrists, he bends forward and to the right, in such a way coming out from the steady position. At that, Uke can't keep the opponent's arm. Using this moment, Tori catches the adversary's neck from behind by the right hand, and takes his right arm behind the spine by the left one. Tori finishes his hold by putting the right knee under the adversary's bending head and by further controlling Uke.

456

457   458   459

Tatsumaki
(fig. 460-463)

The opponents are in front of each other in the standing positions. Uke makes the step forward by the left leg and synchronously with it he catches the adversary's heteronymous arms by his hands.

Tori doesn't give a possibility to finish the grip of his arms completely. Acting for advance, he spreads fingers and raises his hands up. In this position the adversary's grip is not strong and "finished". At this moment he moves his left leg towards the opponent, lowers on the tatami, extends his right leg forward and throws Uke over himself in falling.

460

461   462   463

Gyaku Gasso
(fig.464-467)

The opponents are in front of each other in the standing positions. Uke makes the step forward by the left leg and synchronously with it he catches the adversary's heteronymous arms by his hands. Acting for advance, Tori moves his arms on arcs to the external sides, then up, inside and down. In this position Tori'hands press on Uke wrists top-down. The attacking person feels the strong pain and must release the grip. Tori catches the opponents' arms, keeping his hands and fingers. Then Tori turns to the right and throws the adversary on the tatami.

464

465   466   467

Gokajo
(Review of selected techniques)

Tachiai

Makikomi Kuchiki
(fig.468-471)

The opponents are in front of each other in the standing positions. Uke makes the step forward by the right leg and synchronously strikes the direct blow in the belly by the right fist – Chudan Tsuki. Tori shifts to the left, going away from the attack line. He takes the attacking extremity away by the left arm and catches it near the hand base. Then he catches the adversary's fist from above by the right hand. Tori twists Uke's hand in such a way that his fist rib is directed up and presses his forearm down by the left arm. Strong pain feelings force Uke to lower down on the knees. After that, Tori keeps the adversary on the ground and finishes beating him.

Simoku
(fig.472-475)

The opponents are in front of each other in the standing positions. Uke makes the step forward by the left leg and synchronously with it strikes the descending chopping blow from the right to the left and top-down – Yokomen Uchi. Tori shifts to the left. He blocks the adversary's attack by the right arm and catches the adversary's attacking extremity. Then he bends, catches the opponent's lead leg by the left hand and loads him on himself. Straightening the knees and spine, Tori makes the throw over the shoulders.

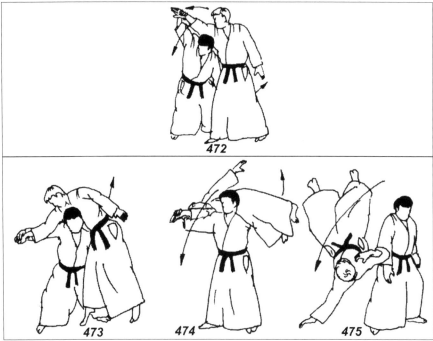

Emono Dori
(fig.476-479)

Uke comes close to Tori (Tori's both arms are as if bound with each other), and catches the adversary's heteronymous arms by both hands. Tori as if coincides with the adversary's actions and redirects his movement to the right. Following his force, Tori turns to the right, takes his arms behind the head and makes Shiho Nage. After that, Tori holds, and finishes beating the adversary.

476

477   478   479

Chapter 4
Aiki no Jutsu
(Review of selected techniques)

Aiki no Jutsu – is an advanced technical section in Daito-ryu Aiki Budo, which study begins only after ten years of Hiden Mokuroku practice. It's very difficult to describe Aiki no Jutsu holds in words, because attention is concentrated on feeling Ki energy here. The section is Kata series, where a practicing person trains to use the adversary's expressed energy for his own. It is usually achieved at the expanse of applying two main principles: Aiki Age (ascending Aiki) and Aiki Sage (descending Aiki). A fighter acquires skills of feeling the least direction of the opponent's force, after which he "borrows" it from him and abruptly puts him down on the tatami. Let's consider several most demonstrative techniques of this section.

Tachiai

Katate dori – Aiki Nage
(480-483)

The opponents are in front of each other in the standing positions. Uke makes the step forward by the right leg and synchronously with it he catches the adversary's heteronymous arms by his hands. Without expecting when the opponent finishes his grip, Tori raises both arms up towards the direction of Uke's movement, demonstrating Aiki Age principle. Then Tori turns to the left. He redirects the adversary's force to the left forward and down by the abrupt movement, in such a way breaking his balance and throwing him down on the tatami.

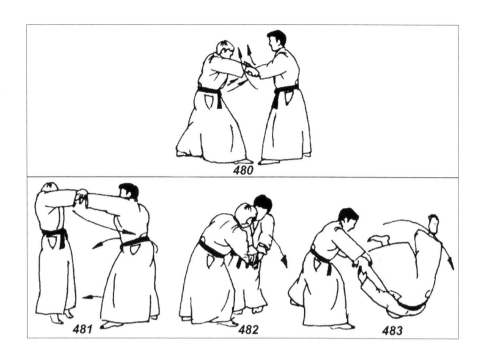

480

481 482 483

Ushiro Ryote dori – Aiki Nage
(fig.484-487)

Uke is in the standing position behind Tori's spine. Uke makes the step forward by and synchronously with it he catches the adversary's heteronymous arms by his hands. Tori doesn't expect when the opponent finishes his grip. Passing a bit ahead of him, he moves forward, taking the opponent with him. Tori rotates the right hand on arc up to the right and down, twisting the opponent's wrist. Then the defending person turns to the left, leaves the right arm behind his spine, and raises the left one on big arc up. Uke tries to keep the grip and finds himself in the extremely unsteady position. Using it, Tori continues to turn to the left, moves the left arm on arc down, directs Ki forward and down, throwing the adversary on the tatami.

484

485   486   487

Kubi Juji-Shime – Aiki Nage
(fig.488-491)

Uke tries to make the suffocating grip Kubi Juji-Shime by both arms. Acting for advance, Tori strikes the short blow on ribs by the fists. Then he dives to the right between the opponent's arms. Using Uke's generated strain, Tori turns to the left, and lowers down, directing Ki to the same side. Uke loses balance and falls on the tatami.

488

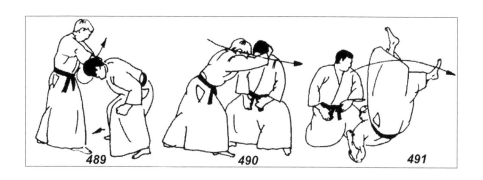

489   490   491

Conclusion

As a conclusion of this book, devoted to the ancient effective style Bujutsu of samurais from Takeda clan, I find it necessary to demonstrate the main conceptions of **Aiki** in **Daitoryu Aikijujutsu** briefly and to note their difference with ones of **Aikido** by Morihei Ueshiba.

Aiki means to pull, when you are pushed, and to push, when you are pulled. It is slowness, including speed and rapidity, which root is in softness, aimed at harmonization of your movement with adversary's **Ki**.

Kiai is opposite to **Aiki** – pushing to the limit, the force, containing even more effort.

Aiki never resists and never opposes more force to the attacking one.

Thus, «**Aiki**» in **Daito-ryu** – is a set of strategic principles of conducting a combat, as opposite to "Energy harmonization" in **Aikido**.

Daito-ryu Aikijujutsu and **Aikido** have differences not only in terms, but also in the final aim of using their holds.

Thus, one, who practices Aikido, tries to force an adversary to leave his aggressive intents by the continuous escape from his attacks, soft throws and holdings. The aim of **Daito-ryu Aikijujutsu** after setting control over an enemy is the instant and complete neutralization of him by a following throw that cannot be prevented by **Ukemi** (safety), or a finishing blow in vitally important points of the human body.

Just this intention to the real martial use gave **Daito-ryu Aikijujutsu** a glory of one of most effective and complex Martial systems of Japan that greatly influenced Budo as a whole throughout the world.

Made in the USA
Middletown, DE
16 July 2023

35247284R00055